Life Cycle of a
Chicken

Angela Royston

Heinemann Library
Des Plaines, Illinois

Designed by Celia Floyd
Illustrations by Alan Fraser
Printed in Hong Kong / China

02 01 00 99
10 9 8 7 6 5 4 3 2

Library of Congress Cataloging-in-Publication Data

Royston, Angela.
    Life cycle of a chicken / by Angela Royston.
        p.   cm.
    Includes bibliographical references and index.
    Summary: Introduces the mating, hatching, life cycle, eating, predators, and lifespan of chickens.
    ISBN 1-57572-698-X (lib. bdg.)
    1. Chickens--Life cycles--Juvenile literature. 2. Leghorns (Poultry)--Life cycles--Juvenile literature. [1. Chickens.]
    I. Title.
    SF487.5.R694   1998
    636.5--dc21   98-10754
                                                                    CIP
                                                                    AC

Acknowledgments
The Publisher would like to thank the following for permission to reproduce photographs:
Bruce Coleman/Jane Burton pp. 9, 12; Heather Angel p. 8; NHPA/William Paton p. 24, NHPA/Manfred Danegger p. 25; Oxford Scientific Films/David Thompson p. 11, Oxford Scientific Films/Michael Leach p. 13, Oxford Scientific Films/G. I. Bernard pp. 26-27; Photo Researchers Inc./Tim Davis p. 10, Photo Researchers Inc./Kenneth H. Thomas pp. 14, 23; Roger Scruton pp. 4, 5, 6, 7, 15, 16, 17, 18, 19, 20, 21, 22.

Cover photograph: Britstock-IFA/Bernd Ducke.

Our thanks to Dr. Bryan Howard, University of Sheffield, in the preparation of this edition.

Contents

Meet the Chickens

Chickens are birds. They have feathers, wings, and a **beak**. Different kinds of chickens have different colored feathers.

Egg   3 weeks   I day old

The chicken in this book is a White Leghorn **cockerel.** He began life inside an egg. The egg was laid by his mother, a White Leghorn hen.

7 weeks

I year

The Eggs are Laid

The mother hen laid the egg in a nest. Every day she lays another egg and now there are six eggs in the nest.

Egg   3 weeks   1 day old

The mother hen sits on the eggs to
keep them warm. Inside each egg
a new chick is growing.

7 weeks

I year

Hatching

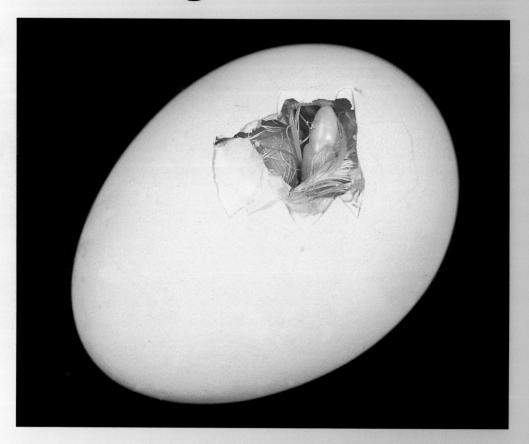

The eggs are beginning to **hatch**. The chick uses its **beak** to chip a hole in the shell.

Egg   3 weeks   1 day old

The chick chips a hole all around
the egg. Now it uses its body to
push the egg apart. The little chick
is wet and tired.

7 weeks

1 year

Very soon its soft, **downy** feathers have dried. The little chick stands up and looks around.

Egg

3 weeks

1 day old

This chick has just **hatched** too.
Soon all the chicks have left the
eggs and are cheeping loudly.

7 weeks

1 year

4 days old

12

The little chicks drink water and eat seeds among the straw. They stay close together and follow the mother hen wherever she goes.

Egg 3 weeks I day old

This chick has been separated from his mother. He listens for his mother clucking and runs after her.

7 weeks

I year

Young Chicken

The chicks are bigger now, but they still shelter under their mother's wing. New, white feathers have grown in place of the yellow **down**.

Egg   3 weeks   I day old

The young **cockerel** has long tail feathers and a red **comb** on top of his head.

7 weeks

1 year

The chickens leave their mother and live in the **chicken run** with the other hens. Here the **cockerel** has flown up onto the fence to have a look around.

16

Egg

3 weeks

I day old

Now he pecks among the grass looking for seeds and worms to eat. He swallows his food whole and it is ground up in a stomach called a **gizzard**.

7 weeks

1 year

Laying Eggs

5 months

The chickens are nearly full grown. This hen sits in one of the egg boxes in the hen house. She clucks loudly and then climbs out.

Egg

3 weeks

1 day old

She has just laid her first egg! From now on she will lay an egg almost every day. Her eggs have not been **fertilized**, so there are no chicks growing inside them.

7 weeks

I year

20

The young **cockerel** struts around the farmyard. He watches carefully over several young hens. If one wanders off, he chases it back.

Egg   3 weeks   I day old

The cockerel protects these hens from danger. If another cockerel comes near one of them, he chases it away.

7 weeks

1 year

22

This hen is ready to **mate**. The young **cockerel** mates with her and **fertilizes** her eggs. She lays the eggs and sits on them.

Egg

3 weeks

1 day old

The eggs have **hatched** and there is a new **brood** of chicks. The hen looks after them, but the cockerel keeps a close eye on them too.

7 weeks

1 year

Danger!

Very early one morning a fox climbs into the **chicken run**. He is a predator. At first the chickens do not see him.

Egg   3 weeks   1 day old

The fox grabs a hen. The **cockerel** and the other chickens squawk and flap, but the fox jumps out of the chicken run and hurries away.

7 weeks

I year

The Farmyard

The cockerel has a busy life. He watches over the hens and chicks and from time to time he crows loudly.

He will stay on the farm until he dies. He may live until he is about ten years old, if the fox doesn't catch him.

Life Cycle

Eggs

1

Hatching

2

Chick

3

Young Chicken

4

5

Cockerel

Fact File

A hen lays between 100 and 300 eggs a year, but not more than one a day.

The shell forms around the egg inside the hen's body. It takes about a day for the egg to form before it is ready to be laid.

People have kept chickens for over 3,000 years. They collect their eggs and eat them.

Chickens are probably the most common bird in the world. There are more than 10 billion (10,000,000,000) of them.

Glossary

beak hard covering of a bird's mouth

brood a group of birds that hatch at
the same time

chicken run an area of fenced-in
ground near a hen house

cockerel a young male chicken

comb a fleshy red crest on the top of
a chicken's head

down soft feathers

fertilizes a female egg is fertilized when
it joins with a sperm from a male

gizzard a special stomach for grinding
up food before it passes into the
chicken's second stomach

hatch to be born out of an egg

mate when a male and a female come
together to produce babies

More Books to Read

Back, Christine. *Chicken and Egg.* Parsippany, NJ: Silver Burdett Press. 1991.

Legg, Gerald & Salariya, David. *From Egg to Chicken.* Danbury, CT: Watts, Franklin Inc. 1998.

Stone, Lynn. *Chickens.* Vero Beach, FL: Rourke Corp. 1990.

Index